HOMES
& GARDENS
LIBRARY OF
INTERIORS

Living Rooms

HOMES & GARDENS

LIBRARY OF INTERIORS

Living Rooms

Amanda Harling

PAVILION

To M and M

First published in Great Britain in 1996 by
Pavilion Books Ltd
26 Upper Ground
London SE1 9PD

Copyright © Pavilion Books 1996
Photographs copyright see page 96
Designed by Peter Bennett
Picture research by Emily Hedges

The moral right of the publisher has been asserted.

A CIP catalogue record for this book is available from the British Library.

ISBN: 1 85793 784 8

Typeset in Gill Sans Medium
Printed and bound in Spain by Bookprint

10 9 8 7 6 5 4 3 2 1

This book may be ordered by post direct from the publisher.
Please contact the Marketing Department.
But try your bookshop first.

Contents

Introduction

Successful living rooms come in all shapes, sizes and colours – as can be seen in the pages of this book. Yet one factor they all have in common is the sense of comfort. Imbued with vitality and warmth, they are the sort of rooms that one longs to find at the end of a long journey.

Pleasing to the eye and in their own small way uplifting to the spirit.

There are philistines who claim to be oblivious to their domestic surroundings, but most of us are acutely aware of whether or not we like the design of a room. One only has to think of the vast budgets that interior designers have at their disposal to realize that the business of making people feel comfortable and happy is taken very seriously indeed by those whose livelihoods depend on it; hoteliers, restaurateurs and club owners spring to mind. Fortunately most of us are in the position of having only our own modest house, cottage or flat to do up but the principle remains the same – the more inviting and commodious a

room, the more it is enjoyed – by owners and guests alike.

Good interior design is not dependent on money. Having been involved in the world of design and decoration for most of my life, I have been privileged to see within innumerable private homes – some vast, some minuscule. Whilst many of those verging on the palatial have clearly had a king's ransom lavished upon them, there is never any guarantee that these glitzy houses will be deemed worthy of being written about or photographed – acres of marble and gold taps are not what magazine editors are looking for. Homes that have been decorated with verve and imagination are infinitely preferable and they

are undoubtedly the most difficult to find. These examples of stylish interior decoration are even more difficult to define. They have an immediate visual impact: sometimes due to grandeur but more frequently as a result of a unique fusion of colour, scale and comfort.

Over the past ten years or so there has been a phenomenal growth of interest in interior design. Whereas it was formerly considered to be the domain of the wealthy, home interest magazines and television programmes have done much to increase the general awareness of design for the home. Terence Conran and Laura Ashley were also hugely instrumental, in their very different ways, in bringing style to the high street.

Large department stores devote ever-increasing amounts of floor space to furniture and home accessories and they can be an excellent source of ideas and inspiration. Don't limit your window-shopping to the large stores, as the small specialist retailer will have a much wider range to choose from and should offer a far greater level of expertise when it comes to advising you on design as well as technical details.

Blending the disparate elements of interior design into a home that reflects your individuality is an exciting challenge. On the following pages you will find rooms decorated in a wide range of styles, which will help you to define your own personal preferences. You will also come across numerous inventive ideas that can be adapted to your own particular circumstances. The extensive directory at the back of the book should be of help in the search for suppliers, manufacturers and retailers of decorative furniture, fabrics and accessories.

Anyone in possession of a credit card can furnish a living room, but to instil character and individuality requires something more — confidence in your own inimitable taste. You can of course opt out of the challenge of doing it all yourself by engaging an interior designer. But why miss out on the fun? Take on the project yourself and become immersed in the irresistible world of colour, design and decoration. It is, after all, a subject that has engrossed the

civilized world for generation after generation.

Having confidence in your own judgement is essential. A wonderful idea can so easily be diluted into pallid compromise by those who don't share your vision. Study books on decoration. Look at paintings and notice how they are framed. Visit not only museums but the great houses in your area and beyond. Compare the work of interior designers. Analyse those features which you think make or break a room. Build up a file of magazine and newspaper cuttings that you find particularly interesting and inspiring. If there's an aspect of design that you become passionate about, think about incorporating it into the decoration of the room (as has the owner of the East Anglian cottage illustrated on page 37). It will prove to be enormous fun and who knows, you might soon find yourself inundated with commissions from admiring friends.

While some of the living rooms shown in these pages are the work of professional interior designers, many have been created by their accomplished but entirely amateur owners. The methods with which these imaginative and individual rooms have been put together varies enormously, as do characteristics such as architectural style, size, layout and so on. Though a sense of traditionalism is evident in most of the rooms, it is traditionalism with a distinctly contemporary edge. There are absolutely no museum pieces and no stately homes — but over a hundred very comfortably lived-in rooms — each and every one a source of inspiration.

Style

Deciding upon a style of decoration that is both appropriate for the room and pleasing to the eye is the most important part of any interior design project. Careful consideration must be given to this critical aspect right from the beginning, as it is not something that can easily or cheaply be rectified halfway through the exercise. Though it can be tempting to take advantage of a bargain, it is generally a better idea to wait until you know roughly what look you are aiming for before you venture forth armed with a cheque book. While it's easy to relegate an unsuitable item of clothing to the local charity shop, getting rid of an ill-chosen three-piece suite can prove rather more problematical.

In these stylistically anarchic times, choosing a style or styles of decoration can be a bewildering process. Set aside time to work out what types of interiors you find particularly pleasing. It might help to jot down a few notes with a description of your ideal room. Do you like the sparseness of minimal decoration — white walls, little furniture and a feeling of space, or do you feel happier surrounded with colour and pattern? Perhaps you find yourself attracted to the clean, uncompromising lines of modern furniture, or maybe you feel that a combination of antique, contemporary and ethnic pieces holds more appeal.

The architectural period of the building often provides a useful reference point from which to start planning. An existing feature of a room, such as an inglenook fireplace, might suggest the gleam of dark furniture and richly textured fabrics. A solid wood-block floor might point you in the direction of a more contemporary style where natural materials and neutral colours work so well together. While there is no reason

to stick rigidly to that period's style of decoration, it often helps to bear in mind the nature and scale of the building when deciding what sort of furniture to choose, leading to a harmonious final result. Developing a basic knowledge of general decorative styles will prove invaluable, enabling you to make informed decisions regarding the choice of fabrics, colours and furniture in addition to the innumerable other details that contribute to the making of a successful living room. It also prevents basic mistakes being made, such as introducing inappropriate materials and designs into period rooms.

Traditional-style rooms come in many guises but the principal elements – fabrics, wall colours, furniture and accessories – are based on period designs. There has never been such a wide variety of merchandise available in as many period styles as there is now. Having settled on a style of decoration that you think is suitable for your home and your way of life, don't feel duty-bound to throw out existing furniture even if it is of the wrong period. Furniture has always been passed down through the generations and it is through combining furniture, paintings and fabrics of different periods that some of the most successful rooms evolve. A particular architectural or decorative style can be created in any number of ways – using the wall colour, the fabric design, the period details such as panelling, window design, fireplace design or a curtain treatment. While authentic period pieces add character to the room, think carefully about the seating – oak settles may be in keeping with sixteenth and seventeenth-century style but they are not comfortable.

Similarly, Georgian sofas are beautiful but can be unyielding and rather formal in appearance. A contemporary sofa made in a traditional style will certainly prove more comfortable, and when covered in a fabric of the chosen period it will help to contribute a sense of period style to the room. Learn to identify the particular characteristics of the period you're interested in, so that when you come to buy furniture you will be able to assess immediately whether the piece

is of the period and style that you're looking for. The advantage of this approach can be seen around some of the best dinner tables: sets of period dining chairs are notoriously expensive but it is often possible to pick up a fine single chair for a modest outlay. A collection of chairs of roughly the same period, perhaps differing slightly in tone, style and size, will co-exist quite happily round the table, whereas the effect of a group of widely differing styles is confusing.

When embarking upon the decoration of any period property, the key point to remember is whether the style is appropriate or not. To install Corinthian columns in a working man's terraced cottage, or replace sash windows with aluminium frames would be sacrilegious. Many people are now replacing architectural details such as cornices, deep skirting boards, panelled doors and fireplaces which were ripped out in the decades after the war when modernism ruled over aesthetic considerations. It is now generally accepted that the basic architectural

proportions of Georgian, Victorian and Edwardian houses had been refined to a point which is difficult to improve upon. This appreciation of our heritage has even been extended to paint manufacturers, who now go to great pains to reproduce authentic period colours. Even the earlier types of paint, such as distemper, are once again proving popular.

Our temperate climate strongly influences our way of life – pale, watery daylight is much better suited to interiors furnished with subdued and muted colours. Even in these days of central heating and air conditioning, most of us still consider an open fire to be a highly desirable feature in living rooms. As icy draughts are also very much part of the British way of life, it seems likely that the insulating qualities of heavy, interlined curtains will ensure that this quintessential feature of traditional style will be with us for the foreseeable future. However, the frilled, flounced extravaganzas that billowed into fashion a decade or so ago have now given way to less grandiose window treatments that are more in keeping with the general movement towards a simpler, 'less is more' lifestyle.

We still love to mix the exotic with the antique. The English-country-house look partly owes its origins to our travelling, trading forefathers. Lacquerwork, ceramics and porcelain from China, cottons and silks from India, rugs from the Middle East, paintings, sculpture and fine furniture from Italy and France – all were imported into Britain in vast quantities during the seventeenth, eighteenth and nineteenth centuries, leading to permanent changes in our notions of style. Over the last hundred years or so, design movements such as Arts and Crafts, Art Deco and Modernism have strongly influenced our domestic surroundings. Currently, as the vogue for simpler interiors

continues, the work of innovative young British designers is finding an appreciative home market.

Bearing in mind the uses to which the room will be put helps to define a style that will be pleasing as well as practical. If small children are likely to be around, you will probably do better to postpone the use of finer fabrics until the danger of self-expression with crayons and jelly is past. If you propose to use the room for work as well as play, take into account at the initial stages the requirement for a desk or table adequate for your needs. Trying to fit in a large piece of furniture at a later stage often proves unsatisfactory, as the balance of the room is destroyed.

The living rooms shown in the following section are furnished and decorated in a wide variety of styles ranging from rustic informality to stark minimalism. All are highly individual and resist strict categorization, but in each case the finished result successfully enhances the characteristics of that particular room.

Although informal and unpretentious, this living room is decorated with great individual style, redolent of Horace Walpole's Gothick extravaganza at Strawberry Hill. The fireside chair and the chest of drawers are of different though complementary styles, ensuring that the room is not just a pastiche. The fireplace, with its decorative elements highlighted in strawberry-red paint, sets the tone for this unusual and colourful interpretation of Gothick style.

14

The sculptural qualities of wrought iron are a strong decorative feature in this contemporary living room. In addition to the staircase, which rises through the house, a low glass-topped coffee table is designed along the same spare lines. White walls and a well-upholstered white sofa recall the all-white rooms created by the Edwardian decorator Syrie Maugham, but in this case accents of strong blues and yellows have been introduced. The result is uncluttered and elegant.

A contemporary interpretation of a classical Georgian interior is illustrated in this strongly coloured blue and yellow sitting room. The fine proportions of the room are emphasized by dividing the walls into symmetrical panels and highlighting the mouldings in white paint. A yellow of such strength would not have been used during the period, but, teamed with the black fireplace and the bright blue of the sofas and rug, the choice appears entirely appropriate.

Some rooms are clearly and unashamedly dedicated to luxurious comfort, and this certainly is such a room. The clotted-cream colour of the walls, curtains, sofa and carpet emphasizes the feeling of space. The note of luxury is established at the moment of entry by the vision of extravagant nineteenth-century-style swags and tails of the curtain treatment for the wide bay window. Opulent and costly in this case, such a style is not beyond even quite modest budgets.

Left: A mixture of textures, patterns and soft, muted colours gives this room a cosy, Victorian feeling. The comfort and display associated with traditional living rooms is manifest – a deep-seated chintz-covered armchair mixes happily with a more rugged pair covered in leather. Above: This beautiful, nineteenth-century room has been given an open, contemporary feeling by painting the walls a pale hyacinth blue and leaving the windows free of curtains.

Left: The colour combination of blue and cream is typical of traditional Scandinavian decoration, and the style of this living room is similarly cool, classical and restrained. The trompe-l'oeil panels on the walls add interest and highlight the fine architectural proportions of the room. Above: By providing little in the way of distraction, muted shades of cream and white have been used to create a sophisticated setting for this beautifully displayed but understated collection of oriental artefacts.

Decorative textiles have been used to great effect in this warm and welcoming country sitting room. With so many gorgeous patterns to study, one is scarcely aware of the white painted walls and ceiling, but it is that plain background that stops the room from appearing claustrophobic. Each and every pattern used in this sitting room is different, but the final result is far from confusing to the eye, due to the tonal similarity of the colours.

There is nothing twee about the decoration of this living room in a West Country cottage. In order to increase the feeling of space in what was formerly a cramped, poky couple of rooms, the original boxed-in staircase was removed and replaced with one of a more open design. White-painted walls and ceiling reflect light into the room and provide an uncluttered background for the patterned blue and white fabrics used for upholstery and curtains.

Left: A simple brushwood garland seen hanging above the wood-burning stove sums up the charm and character of a cosy, unpretentious country living room. Above: Equipped with a practical wood-burning stove, the large fireplace is the natural focal point in this informal country sitting room. Casually but confidently thrown together, it is furnished with a well-worn collection of antiques mixed with contemporary paintings and ceramics. A kelim rug adds a vibrant note of colour to the flagstone floor.

Top: Austerity allied with comfort is the keynote of this highly mannered room with its oriental overtones and eye-catching elements. The simple yet rather grand bureau with its quietly spectacular cupboard is set between a pair of handsome Indian paintings and a boldly contemporary Chinese folding screen. Above: The pale airy sitting room of this 1830s house in Bath is furnished with a cherrywood table and bookcase made by the owner, cabinet-maker Ed McFadden.

An interesting room which combines the best elements of tradition and modernism. At first glance this appears to be a rather austere living room, an impression deriving from the unusual design of the sofa, which makes its own link between Victorian deep-cushioned comfort and the spare modern lines of the frame – a modernism that is echoed in the shape of the coffee table. A pair of Regency elbow chairs adds to the duality of the overall concept in the same way as the softly gathered curtains.

Property developer Sara May converted a former office unit into a compact one-bedroomed home. The focal point of the plain, white-painted room was created by the hanging, a vibrantly coloured painting by Mark Wigan in the centre of the main wall. The highly eclectic mix of contemporary, antique and ethnic furniture and accessories subsequently chosen for the room reflect the colours in the painting. A sense of order is imposed by the arrangement of the furniture.

A serenely splendid Regency sofa upholstered in mattress ticking is the focal point in this symmetrical arrangement of furniture in the living room of an 1840s London house. The pale buff colour of the walls was picked from a colour in the pretty, striped curtains bought at a London antique market. A pair of strikingly modern low-voltage standard lamps casts light at either end of the sofa, and portrait cushions from Timney Fowler add an amusing contemporary touch.

Below: Windows can be the most assertive element in any interior setting, and certain windows – from Gothick to great modern spaces – can become arbiters of the decoration within. This is especially true of windows that offer unusual or even spectacular vistas beyond – as seen here. For such breathtaking scenes, the 'less is more' philosophy has substantial appeal. Right: Minimal chic – a chair, a desk, a window, and little else except light, space and the warm colour of a wood-strip floor.

Colour, Pattern

Colour has the most profound influence on the atmosphere of any room, but with a vast

array of papers, paints and fabrics to choose from it is a subject that can

seem bewilderingly complex. Reaction to colour, combinations of

colour, patterns and texture deeply affect the way we feel.

Some make us feel secure, others make us initially optimistic but pall after a short time.

There seem to be innumerable variations with few set rules. Some people have a natural eye for

the fine gradations of colour, others can barely detect the difference between yellow and ochre. Close

observation and experience are invaluable in taming this most subjective of areas. Certain colours and patterns are

associated with specific periods and styles of decoration. In many cases this is due to the availability of pigments at

the time in question. Until the middle of the nineteenth century, when a great many of the more difficult colours

were made synthetically, the range was fairly limited. Moreover, the quality of commercially available pigments was

nowhere near as dependable as we have come to take for granted today. The result,

however, was often to produce the most subtle and natural texture full of imperfections,

which gave such character to these period decorative schemes — something that no

modern vinyl or latex can achieve despite its stability, washability and durability.

During the sixteenth century, the predominant colours used in tapestries and crewel-work were the muted shades

of blues, greens, earthy reds and ochres obtained through using natural dyes. Rooms would have been wood-panelled

or decorated with patterns or images painted onto roughly plastered walls. Rich, jewel-like colours, such as deep

& Texture

reds, blues and greens, suited the ornate grandeur of the baroque style in the latter part of the seventeenth century. During the early part of the eighteenth century the French rococo style was associated with pale pinks, blues, yellows and greens and the plentiful use of mirror and gilt, further adding to the effect of lightness and elegance. Also typical of that time were *toile de Jouy* fabrics with their amusing depictions of bucolic country scenes. The Regency period, which broadly spans the end of the eighteenth century and the beginning of the nineteenth century, was characterized by forthright colours often combined in stripes. In particular this period will always be associated with the colour red, which was extensively used to convey the luxury and liveliness of the times. Decorative painting such as marbling and graining was very much in vogue and the relative cheapness of its execution, in comparison with the wonderful richness of colour and texture it produced, made it extremely popular. Brighton Pavilion or the Soane Museum in Lincoln's Inn Fields in London are excellent sources of inspiration if you find strong and unusual colours appealing. Well-to-do Victorians considered themselves pillars of a solid and respectable Establishment, and their homes reflected this gravitas. Furniture and fabrics of a frivolous nature were consigned to the attic, and reception rooms became repositories for vast amounts of dark-brown furniture and heavily fringed, sombre fabrics. The intricate and beautifully balanced designs of William Morris, the leading exponent of the Arts and Crafts Movement, are still produced by Sandersons – ideal for creating an instant impression of late-Victorian style. The interest in period

style continues unabated — wallpaper and fabric manufacturers add new designs to their collections each season,

but the theme or principal motif is more often than not adapted from a classical or traditional design. Some companies

produce no new designs, merely re-colouring patterns from their archive collection to fit in with the current vogue.

One constant running through all these periods is the fact that white has rarely been used in the decoration of

interiors, with the exception of ceilings, which were often tinted with red or blue

anyway. However, during the latter half of this century, especially in the

field of contemporary design, white has become much more popular.

The direction in which your living room faces will have an

important bearing on which colour you choose for the walls. Rooms with a northerly

aspect often appear to be lacking in warmth, so you might compensate for this by using a

sunny yellow or ochre. Cooler, lighter colours such as off-whites, pale greens, yellows and blues can

work especially well in rooms facing south and enjoying plentiful natural light. Attempting to make small, dark

rooms appear lighter through the use of white or off-white is generally a mistake; the lack of natural light will result

in the room feeling merely dull and colourless. An alternative course of action would be to use a deep red or green

to imbue the room with a sense of warmth and drama. Add bookshelves, good lighting and strongly coloured

curtains, and you have the makings of cosy library-cum-living room.

It is a far easier task to match wall colour to fabric than the other way round. Study

the constituent colours of the fabric closely; you might find that one of the less dominant

colours proves ideal for the walls. Curtains and walls are always adjacent; when the

colours bear a close relationship to each other the effect is generally pleasantly harmonious. An increasing number

of specialist companies now produce ranges of historically accurate colours, using traditional methods and

materials to achieve an authentic finish. They may be more expensive but, although similar colours are to be found in mass produced modern paints, they lack the depth of colour and inimitable texture of paint produced using traditional methods and natural pigments.

By using broken colour it is possible to add a softer, more natural appearance to wall surfaces and furniture. In nature, uniform coloration is a totally unknown phenomenon. If a child is asked to paint a tree, the leaves are

always depicted as one shade of green and the trunk is brown. In reality, however a leaf is many shades of green, just as the trunk is rarely brown but a mixture of greys and greens. If the subject of decorative paint finishes is new to you, try experimenting with sample-size pots of two similar shades of the same colour. You will be amazed at the sense of depth and movement that can be added to a flat surface by applying the paint in different ways. For instance, by painting a thinned-down mixture of one colour over the other, a two-tone effect is immediately produced. Or use a brush to drag down vertically for a gently striated look. There are numerous books available on the subject that will explain the processes involved in more detail.

It is important not to underestimate the significance of texture in the overall decorative scheme. Without the interplay of light and shadow on a variety of surfaces an otherwise stunning room can appear lifeless and dull. Sisal, coir and jute floor coverings with their rich textural qualities look equally at home in traditional and contemporary settings. For those who prefer the softness of conventional carpet, several manufacturers now produce ranges that imitate the appearance of coir matting. Rugs and dhurries can be used to introduce an element of pattern as well as texture and are also useful for the way that they help to define a particular part of a room – such as the fireside or the seating area. The textural qualities of different fabrics varies enormously – as can be seen if you compare the effect of sunlight shining on the surface of silk, cotton and velvet – and can have a significant influence on the appearance of a room.

Below: The owner of this London house used primary colours of red, yellow and blue to make a bold statement in this handsomely proportioned living room. Sunny yellow walls and the russety tones of the wooden floorboards ensure that the room glows with warmth on even the gloomiest winter day. Plain white curtains add to the feeling of space by reflecting light back into the room. Right: Another view of this colourful room furnished in an eclectic mixture of styles.

33

The combination of colour, texture and pattern convey an atmosphere of cosy sophistication in this sitting room containing a fine collection of satinwood Biedermeier furniture. The light sheen of the lustrous ochre-coloured wall finish provides an effective backdrop for the pictures, ornaments and red and ochre curtain fabric. As always, the natural texture and colour of coir floor covering proves the perfect foil for the patterns and colours of an oriental rug.

A wall finish in tones of pale golden-yellow distemper adds a sense of warmth to this formal London drawing room. The other colours in the room are based on those of the woven green, cream and red fabric chosen to cover the sofas and the pair of boldly striped silk cushions, giving the room a striking, yet homogeneous look. Plain, undyed silk taffeta curtains are trimmed with tassels and braid in deep red, a colour combination echoed in the bordered rug that defines the seating area.

Blue and yellow is a classic colour combination, which works well in this cosy, unpretentious country sitting room where the cool tones of the carpet and sofa are balanced by the deep egg-yolk yellow walls. A collection of silhouettes hung in a symmetrical arrangement to one side of the stone fireplace adds interest to the room, as do the antique needlework cushions. The mantelpiece arrangement, though simple, is beautifully balanced, with the *trompe l'oeil* adding a decorative touch.

Right: A rich mix of Mediterranean colours creates a feeling of *joie de vivre* in this airy London flat. Lofty, off-white walls provide a muted backdrop for hot spicy shades of reds, pinks and terracotta. Luminous lilac blue cotton covering the sofa and chair adds a sharp note of contrast. Below: Though refurbished on a limited budget, the style and sophistication of this room are largely due to the bold use of colour. Brilliant bright green walls emphasize the outline of a curvaceous purple sofa.

The paintings of Bloomsbury Group artists Vanessa Bell, Duncan Grant and Roger Fry inspired the owner of this East Anglian cottage to take up the paintbrush himself — with dazzling results. A total disregard for convention has resulted in a series of informal, colourful rooms. The manner in which each of the walls has been roughly painted in a different colour and then hung with a profusion of prints, drawings and collages cleverly obscures the lack of architectural details.

This London living room illustrates how pale colours can work well in rooms blessed with lofty proportions and plenty of natural light. Muted shades of cream, fawn and white are contrasted by the ebonized Regency dining chairs, the splendidly ornate gilt mirror and the marble fireplace. The gently gathered plain cream curtains soften the outline of the two floor-to-ceiling windows and, by being tied back into graceful folds, they avoid making the windows appear too austere.

A colour combination of cream and pink was chosen for this country sitting room. The room receives little natural light but the atmosphere created by the soft, warm colours and the muted patterns is restful and welcoming. Contrast and interest are provided by the pine fireplace and the unusual *faux*-bamboo pedimented bookcase, which fits neatly into the broad, arched alcove. The delicately pleated silk lampshades add to the room's feminine appeal.

The rich red-and-gold colour scheme used in this flat detracts from the modest dimensions of the room. Inspiration for the unusual wall finish came from the patterned French curtain fabric – a burgundy and ochre wool weave acquired at an antique fair. The walls were painted in a gold base colour, followed by two shades of red. After each stage the surface was rubbed down in order to remove some of the paint and create an impression of texture and depth.

Far from being oppressive, the deep red wallpaper and red lampshades give this tiny sitting room-cum-library an atmosphere of warmth and merriment. Though furnished very much in the traditional manner with mahogany bookcases, wing chairs, club fender and ancestral portrait, the effect is lightened by a contemporary upholstery fabric boldly checked in tones of red and yellow. The pale, natural colours of the carpet and the patterned rug also give the room a more modern feel.

By using a colour scheme based predominantly on shades of earthy reds and browns, harmony of colour, pattern and texture has been skilfully achieved in this European living room. The gradation of brown ranges from the deep conker of the window frames and door, and the tawny variations in the wood floor, to the pale tan of the patterned wallpaper. The sofa, covered in a fine red-and-cream stripe, is framed by the stronger colours and design of the curtain fabric.

4

Since Georgian times, dark red has been considered an excellent colour against which to hang fine paintings – in this case of equestrian subjects. In this comfortable, traditionally furnished living room there is a strong contrast between the deep raspberry-red wall finish and the pristine white paintwork of the arched alcove and the white marble fire surround. The sofa upholstered in cream striped fabric is bedecked with a colourful array of cushions, providing yet more contrast.

The walls of this musical living room have been painted a soft shade of hyacinth blue, highlighted by a chalky white ceiling and dado. Although blue is generally thought of as being a cold colour, this shade with its hint of violet gives the room an air of tranquillity rather than coolness. The russet tones of the oak strip-floor add warmth, as do the earthy colours seen in the oriental rug. The highly polished black surface of the grand piano adds to the understated sense of individuality.

47

The pale grey-green walls of this uncluttered modern apartment would seem cold if not balanced by the earthy tones of yellow ochre and burnt sienna used for the upholstery of the armchairs. The expanse of oak strip- flooring adds more warmth to the colour scheme, as do the exposed wood of the window frames and the slats of the blinds. The gleaming brasswork set into the antique chest adds a decorative touch to this restrained, though colourful interior.

46

Left: Age and climate have softened the dramatic effect of this unusual colour combination consisting of upper walls painted an intense turquoise and lower walls palest blue. Although this simply furnished 'sala de estar' is in an old Spanish house, the strong colours could look equally striking in a more northerly climate. Above: The old saying 'red and green should never be seen' is proved wrong in this case. A fiery red carpet adds theatrical strength to the celadon green walls and the floral curtains.

Right: The height of this unusual, vaulted sitting room is emphasized by painting the area above the picture rail white, while the pale shade of green chosen for the lower part of the walls provides an ideal background colour for the decorative pair of Chinese watercolours on the far wall. Warmth and pattern have been introduced by way of the richly patterned fabric on the sofa. Below: Yards of flowered chintz stand out against the plain pastel walls and carpet in this softly coloured country-style room.

Space

Whatever the size of your home, you will want to make the most of the space. Your

first priority therefore is to make an accurate floorplan. Without one,

every decision you make will be based on guesswork, inevitably

leading to a series of unsatisfactory compromises on both

the design and technical aspects of the project. Even the mathematically challenged

should be able, with the help of a friend holding the other end of the tape, to measure the

length, breadth and height of the room. Draw a rough sketch showing the general shape of the room

and enter the measurements on the sketch. Measure every architectural detail in the room – height and width of

fireplace, alcove sizes, chair-rail height, the width and direction in which doors open – it's often possible that just

by re-hanging a door on the opposite side, 75cm/30in or more of wall space can be gained.

Then, having invested in a scale ruler, make a carefully measured plan and elevations of the area. Interior designers

generally use a scale of 1:50, which is considered adequate since it allows space to show

the exact position of small details such as power points and light switches. Once you are

satisfied that the plan is accurate, make several photocopies. They will prove invaluable, as

you can supply the plumber, electrician and carpenter with an exact plan of where you

want things positioned. Don't be tempted to leave the decisions up to them for their only concern is to do the job

quickly, get paid and move onto the next one. Getting tradespeople to come back to rectify a mistake is almost always

difficult, but getting them to accept that the fault is theirs, and the cost should be theirs also, is well nigh impossible.

Once the scale floorplan and elevations are complete you will be able to calculate how best to use the available floor and wall area of the room. Any furniture that you already have should be measured so that scale cut-outs can be made; then, putting out of your mind how the room was arranged previously, move the symbols around on the plan until you find the position that suits you and the layout of the room. You will find that various configurations of furniture are possible in even the smallest of living rooms. Even if you think you have plenty of space, think long and hard before crowding your living room with furniture. A massive three-piece suite might look great in a furniture store the size of an aircraft hangar, but a conventional living room will be swamped by several items of

furniture covered in identical fabric. You could start off with the sofa and see whether chairs in a different style, covered in a complementary fabric, would look less imposing.

Begin by deciding where the seating area should be. If you have a fireplace, the chances are that you will want to locate sofas and chairs within its vicinity. Then work out what other activities need to be planned for. Do you plan to use the room for work or study? Should it be child-proof with space for high-spirited fun and games? Do you need shelf space for books and ornaments? Will there be a television in the room? Do you need good daylight for needlework or painting?

Taking these requirements into account at the planning stage helps you to organize the space so that the room can accommodate its multifarious roles in a functional, orderly manner. Once the seating plan has been decided upon, this will dictate the positions of things such as power and lighting points, wall light heights, radiator locations and television socket – all vital information that is needed before decoration can begin. Also bear in mind how much floor space an average-sized person needs to manoeuvre between pieces of furniture. Failure to plan leads to chaotic, uncomfortable arrangements where valuable floor space is lost unnecessarily to bulky afterthoughts. Incorporating storage space

into the living room from the outset will pay dividends for years to come. Personal possessions and general family clutter accumulate at an alarming rate even in the tidiest of homes, but if they are tucked away out of sight the room doesn't become dominated by the unsightly piles of toys, games and videos that are part of everyday life. Alcoves either side of the chimney breast often make ideal combined storage and display areas. Turn the lower part into cupboards and use the upper section for books and ornaments. If the alcove recess is deep enough, use the space for the television and hi-fi equipment.

Try to avoid one seating area becoming over-sized. While three-seater sofas are proportionally correct for larger rooms, bear in mind that three people will rarely feel comfortable sitting cheek by jowl in a row, unless they already know each other well and are relaxed in each other's company. As a general rule, seating more than eight people in one group tends to make the room feel rather like a waiting room, so if you

have a spacious room, organizing the seating into more intimate groups will create a cosier atmosphere. Such arrangements, where people can move easily from one group to another, are ideal for informal family gatherings – grown-ups can chat amongst themselves, whilst keeping an eye on the antics across the room!

The double reception rooms typical of Georgian and Victorian terraced houses lend themselves perfectly to multi-functional roles. If you work at home, turn one half of the room into an office-cum-library with bookshelves and cupboards lining the walls, while the other half can be kept for the relaxed entertaining of friends. Use a central table as a desk, which, when occasion demands, can also double as a dining table. Alternatively, if space allows, try placing a table in the archway between the two halves of the room. Loaded with books and flowers, the table will mark the division between the seating areas, as well as providing a surface for homework or letter-writing. If the

living room is to be multi-functional, make sure the furniture is, too. Invest in a desk fitted with filing drawers, so that when the working day is over papers can be stored away. Upholstered stools fitted with an integral storage compartment for files and papers can double up as coffee tables, while purpose-made circular chipboard tables will conceal a television and video when covered with a tablecloth.

Certain styles of furniture appear to take up less space than they actually do. Wicker sofas and chairs provide a light, natural-looking alternative to conventional upholstery. Stacking and folding chairs are other useful allies in the

5

quest for space. Other space-enhancing tricks include using the transparent, reflective qualities of glass and perspex wherever practicable. Perspex occasional tables detract little from the spaciousness

of a room, as do glass-topped coffee and dining tables and glass-stemmed lights.

A classic method of increasing the sense of light and space is to use only white or pale colours throughout the room. In theory this works well, but only in rooms that already benefit from plentiful natural light. In practice, no amount of white paint will transform a dark, gloomy basement into an airy expanse. Concentrate instead on giving the room warmth and character with colour, and use mirrors to increase the illusion of space and light. Strips of mirror glass set into the window reveals will make an enormous difference to the quality of light in a dark room, as does hanging a good-sized mirror on the wall facing the window, creating the illusion of a second window.

This is English-country-house decorating on a miniature scale. The narrow sitting room could easily feel cramped, but the combination of a large, uncurtained sash window and a striped yellow-and-cream wallpaper maximizes the feeling of light and space. The profusion of pattern in the furnishing fabrics is balanced by the tonal similarity of the colours – mellow pinks, reds and greens. The *coup de grâce* is provided by the over-sized scale of the antique tapestry.

Below right: Plain white walls and the pale cream fabric used for the curtain and upholstery confer an atmosphere of serenity and spaciousness upon this small but very smart sitting room. The L-shaped seating unit makes excellent use of the limited floor area and also allows space for a large coffee table. Below: Another, more colourful example of an L-shaped seating unit is used to create maximum seating area in the minimum space. The clear glass coffee table is less obtrusive than a solid table would be.

Below: By combining colour, pattern and an over-sized piece of furniture, interior designer Michael Daly has created an atmosphere of exotic grandeur in this small London sitting room. While of an imposing height, the depth of the tall painted cabinet is deceptively shallow so as not to protrude far into the room. A pair of *faux*-bamboo mirrors reflect light back into the room. Right: Another example of how a sizeable piece of furniture can add a sense of importance and drama to a small room.

A French marble fireplace adds architectural gravitas to this elegant sitting room, while an entire wall has been covered in mirror, visually to double the size of the room. The decoration of the room has been kept deliberately simple in order to increase the sense of space still further. The walls and upholstery are of a similar pale shade and just one painting hangs behind the sofa. Cushions, an oriental rug and pretty flowers add bright accents of colour.

Top: This little seaside sitting room is barely bigger than a bathing hut, but it has been furnished with great charm at minimal cost. A fresh coat of white paint and seagrass floor covering are the basic requirements, followed by inexpensive, well-designed wicker armchairs, and gingham cushions. Left: Golden-yellow curtains and walls provide a plain background for the generous proportions of the furniture in this small but confidently furnished living room.

Benefiting from double-aspect windows, the size of this spacious, airy living room has been emphasized by the use of soft pastel colours typical of the eighteenth-century rococo style of decoration. Yellow, blue, taupe, pink and green harmonize against the pale cream background of the walls. The focal point of the room is a magnificent gilded console table; the well-spaced, symmetrical arrangement of pictures above takes full advantage of the generous ceiling height.

A room of this size could easily appear chilly, but the golden-yellow walls convey an atmosphere of warmth, aided and abetted by the contrasting shade of deep-pink fabric chosen for the sofa, and the rich pinks and reds of the Aubusson rug. Furnished with verve and confidence, the central part of the room is occupied by a stretch sofa. The graceful curve of the bow front with its trio of draped French windows makes a fitting backdrop for the grand piano.

The spacious, stone-flagged hallway of this old country house is used also as a sitting area. Many such houses built for the well-to-do during the sixteenth, seventeenth and eighteenth centuries have a fireplace in the hallway, but few have been made as cosy and inviting as this one. An impression of warmth is created solely by the use of red – in many shades. The fabric of the armchair and settle echo the warm pinks and reds of the large rug, while the fireside rug is a deeper red.

Colour has been used sparingly in the small sitting room of this eighteenth-century Dorset cottage to create a roomy, open feeling. By keeping to the colour combination of white and grey-blue an atmosphere of airy lightness is suggested; the use of the same fabric for curtains, sofa and stool reinforces the sense of simple harmony. The classical proportions of the white-painted mantelpiece are complemented by a large gilt overmantel mirror, adding to the impression of light and space.

Although every surface of this friendly sitting room is crammed with furniture and objects, the overall impression is one of spaciousness. The pair of wide French windows that overlook the conservatory undoubtedly contribute to this feeling. The pale uniformity of the wall colour and the well-balanced arrangement of furniture impose a sense of order on an eclectic mixture of styles and fabrics. The vibrant graphic design of the rug gives the impression of elongating the room.

Display

Making the most of your possessions is an art in itself. When shown off with the swagger and pride befitting an Old Master painting, even the humblest of everyday objects can be transformed into a covetable treasure. Insert a favourite photograph into an ornate frame and it will become a source of pleasure – leaving it to moulder in a drawer from one year to the next serves no purpose whatsoever, apart from filling up valuable space.

Books are an essential feature in any living room. As well as a constant source of entertainment and interest, their varied colours and sizes add instant warmth and character. Arranging them in rows, interspersed with small groups of five or six volumes piled one on top of the other, can look more interesting than shelf upon shelf neatly stacked as though part of a municipal library. Alcoves either side of a chimney breast are ideal for built-in bookcases. Shelves can run from floor to ceiling, or the lower part can be designed to provide space for radiators or cupboards.

You may wish to devote some of the shelf space to a display of china or ceramics. If so, consider fitting glass shelves. These will allow light from downlighters installed in the ceiling to filter down, drawing attention to fine detailing and workmanship. An alternative method of highlighting objects on glass shelves is to run strip lights behind the uprights, providing an invisible source of illumination. As alcoves invariably seem to attract a host of electrical equipment – television, hi-fi, computer, reading light and so on – remember to take this into account when drawing up an electrical plan and if possible place the sockets in the cupboards below to hide an unsightly tangle of cables.

Shelving can be free-standing or built-in. If built-in, adding a cornice to the top will make the structure feel more part of the room. Bookcases built over the doorway make the most of every inch of space and will give added importance to the door, but they need to be designed with care if they are not to overwhelm the room. Trimming the shelves with a scalloped leather can look attractive, as can painting the interior of the shelves a contrasting colour to the uprights.

In a living room lacking a fireplace, a generously proportioned bookcase placed at the centre of one wall can provide an important focal point. By placing a sofa between a pair of bookcases, the balanced arrangement provides the focal point towards which furniture in other parts of the room can be directed. Utilize the wall space above the sofa to hang a large picture or mirror, or a selection of smaller pieces. A collection of china plates could provide an alternative form of decoration for the walls. While this is an accepted way of displaying traditional china and fine porcelain, the earthy reds and ochres of Mediterranean pottery look particularly effective in contemporary-style rooms.

Low-cost industrial shelving can be adapted to domestic life, especially in less formal settings. In open-plan living areas, practical steel shelving can be useful for display and storage purposes. As well as helping to divide one area from another visually, its skeletal construction means that it detracts minimally from the feeling of openness that is characteristic of loft apartments and similar spaces.

Choose the objects you wish to display with care. Have confidence in your own taste but be ruthless when it comes to selecting individual pieces. Crowding together a mass of unrelated pieces – even if each is an object of beauty – will not result in a pleasing arrangement. You don't have

to spend a fortune to find interesting items to display. Things like driftwood, stones, shells, pine cones and dried

grasses all have their decorative appeal when imaginatively arranged. Look to yourself for inspiration and analyse

why a particular object, such as a painting or a vase, gives you particular pleasure. Why not build up a collection of

related pieces in the same style? Decide which of your interests you find the most visually

rewarding. Gardening? Needlework? Travel? Cooking? It could even be

stamp collecting. Use that interest to inspire a collection of paintings

or photographs based on one of those favourite themes.

While walls are the obvious surface for displaying pictures, don't hesitate to make a

feature of a striking rug or quilt by hanging it on the wall. After all, needlework panels and

tapestries enhance the walls of many a stately home. As well as being decorative in their own right,

pictures and paintings can be used to define certain features of a room. A focal point such as a chimney breast

provides the perfect backdrop for a stunning arrangement combining wall-hung art with a variety of decorative objects

displayed on the flat surface of the mantelpiece. A collection of identically framed prints or drawings becomes a focal

point when framed and mounted correctly, and can also add a sense of order when hung above a sofa or table.

Symmetry is an important factor in displaying almost anything. A pair of table lamps on a

console table or pairs of obelisks of different sizes are always more pleasing to the eye than

a single item. Similarly, wall sconces hung either side of a mirror give a balanced look to any

wall. Keeping the tops of picture frames on the same horizontal line is also a useful way of

imposing a sense of order on a perhaps otherwise irregular elevation. Hanging a painting in an unconventional position,

such as on the surface of a mirror or the uprights of bookcases, is another way to create a visual impact. Pictures come

in many forms – the only proviso being that the subject should be interesting or decorative, preferably both. If you hanker after a piece of modern art, surprise your friends and maybe yourself with your own creation. One well-known interior designer whose London flat I visited some years ago had made his own version of a painting by a well-known American artist. Visitors to the flat were invariably impressed by how well the designer must have been doing to afford to spend so much on one painting. Old Masters generally take a little longer to copy and the results will probably be less convincing. If, however, you wish to make a feature of one particular painting, there is no more striking way of doing this than lighting it with a concealed projector, which throws light only onto the canvas itself without spilling over onto the surrounding area. Although the projector itself is quite expensive, the ethereal effect of the painting being lit from behind is second to none. If photography is an abiding interest, work on compiling a series of portraits or landscapes that, when enlarged, will form a cohesive collection of your work. You might find that pattern appeals more to you than pictures, so why not frame a sample of fabric or wallpaper – whether it's antique or contemporary is purely a matter of taste.

Cushions, with all their connotations of comfort and relaxation, should play a significant part in the decoration of the living room. The style of the room will dictate whether they are piled high in a profusion of colour and pattern or whether a more precise arrangement, designed to coordinate with other fabrics, is called for.

When chosen with decoration in mind, the colour and beauty of fresh flowers adds a welcoming flourish to any living room. No matter how many floral patterns and motifs a room contains there is never any substitute for the real thing, although dried and silk flowers can be effective – in moderation. Even the smallest jug or vase filled with fresh flowers will add vitality when placed on the mantelpiece as part of an otherwise symmetrical arrangement. Foliage and flowers in a larger container can fill the empty void in the corner of a room. Bold arrangements of dried flowers and leaves in urns and earthenware pots can be used to highlight alcoves and window sills.

A pair of free-standing black bookcases inset into the alcoves either side of the fireplace are filled with a well-ordered arrangement of books interspersed with decorative boxes, baskets and pictures. Above: A fitted bookcase has been incorporated into this dramatic Gothick interior to provide storage space for books, television, hi-fi and an unusual collection of character ceramics. Left: A floor-to-ceiling run of bookshelves frames the doorway in this country sitting room.

When arranged with flair and imagination, books are an effective way to add colour to even the palest room. A floor-to-ceiling bookcase frames the door in this blue and cream living room. By painting the framework of the shelves in shades of blue and green to match the trompe-l'oeil panels on the walls, the bookcase has become an important part of the overall decorative scheme. The deep shelves also contain a varied collection of objects, which contributes to the general air of informality.

Below: Denise Outlaw of Arc Prints has used two classical Piranesi architectural prints with simple black frames to decorate the walls of her South London house. The architectural theme is continued with the stone fragments of Ionic columns displayed on the mantelpiece. Right: Art and nature in tonal harmony – a mantelpiece arrangement of clock and gilded wooden letters is enhanced by the gorgeous colour and shape of these golden parrot tulips.

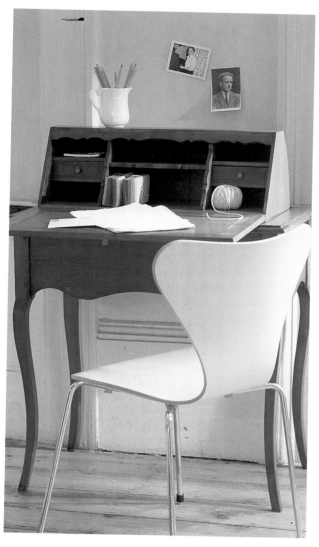

Above: Just the addition of a simple china jug filled with pencils provides a visual flourish to this austere arrangement of an antique wooden desk partnered with a modern plywood pre-formed chair. Left: In the compact Chelsea home of property developer Sara May, this unusual zinc-topped console table doubles as an occasional desk. A pair of torcheres designed by Suzanne Ruggles adds a sense of importance and order to the simple arrangement.

Balance has been imposed on this room by a collection of nine classical prints, displayed to great effect between built-in bookcases and cupboards. The close-hung symmetry of the arrangement has considerably more impact than if the prints were hung singly or in pairs. The classical theme is continued in the miscellany of objects displayed on the trunk — anatomical plaster casts, a bust and a pedimented clock. A light-hearted touch is provided by the hat-bearing cherub.

The asymmetrical layout of this airy London living room is countered by the series of well-balanced arrangements. The pale cream sofa with its pair of dark paisley cushions illustrates the constant interplay of dark and light surfaces that is a feature of the decoration. A pair of tall black table lamps with pleated cream silk shades are placed at either end of the sofa to help define the seating area. The formation in which the four engravings on the far wall are hung accentuates the lofty ceiling height.

Below: The theatrical qualities of red and gold are fully exploited in this fireside arrangement in a flat designed by Michael Daly. The uprights of the wood-grained bookcases have been stencilled in gold to suggest intricate inlay work. The bevelled mirror is flanked by smaller, more ornate brass and gilt frames. A pair of swing-arm wall lights with red and gold adds the final touch. Right: The ruddy hues of the walls, mantelpiece and wooden mirror frame are highlighted by bright green.

Above left: Warm orange walls cast a golden glow over this decorative ensemble arranged by interior designer David Hare on a nineteenth-century *rouge royale* marble mantelpiece. Framed by a tall gilded mirrors the formality of the grouping is softened by the foliage of the orchid. Above: The informal arrangement of roses and mock orange adds to this mantelpiece display. The collection of portraits with its varied shapes, sizes and styles is given cohesion by being hung within a single panel.

Yellow walls, white dado and a strongly coloured red and yellow oriental rug create an appropriately dramatic setting for this highly successful arrangement of furniture and objects of different styles. A pair of simple, provincial chairs, covered in pink *toile de Jouy,* provides a foil for the magnificence of this French commode complete with ornate gilt ornamentation. Two pretty porcelain lamps frame the table-top arrangement of a delicate gilt clock and porcelain cups and saucers.

Glass and gilt add sparkle to this carefully considered arrangement centred around a classical alabaster clock. Textural contrasts abound: the green-painted console table with its gilded decoration; pleated silk shades top the delicate glass stems of the table lamps; the neutral colours of the stone obelisks highlighted by the reflective surfaces of perspex ones; modelled forms in black of a cat, monkey and a hand add strength to this mannered and elegant collection of decorative objects.

Decorative folding screens can also have practical uses. Inspired by eighteenth-century print rooms, this three-panelled screen has been painted an earthy shade of red before being decorated with photocopies of engravings in assorted styles and sizes. As well as screening the room from the draughty hall, the folding screen adds to the visual flamboyance of this richly coloured room, which is decorated in that classical combination of red and yellow.

Above left: A varied collection of furniture, sculpture, paintings and decorative objects is arranged with confidence and originality in this unpretentious living room. Every surface has been used for display but the plain white-painted walls provide a restful backdrop. Above: A colourful collection of cushions fills the gap between sofa and tapestry and adds warmth and comfort. A profusion of summer flowers and greenery in an attractive container provides the finishing touch.

Lighting

Lighting in the living room has two functions – to be decorative as well as practical. In most homes, the room is used at different times of the day for a diverse range of activities. Reading, sewing, watching television, word-processing and entertaining are some of the most usual, and the lighting requirements of each need to be taken into account if the room is to work satisfactorily from morning until night. Flexibility is the key word to remember when it comes to deciding how the room is to be lit, and careful planning is essential if unsightly wires are to be chased into the walls, or hidden below floorboards or behind skirting boards, before the room is decorated.

For the room to adapt to its multi-purpose role, instal a combination of the following types of lighting.

Background or indirect lighting. Switched on from the door to provide a reasonable level of light throughout the room.

Display or accent lighting. Focuses attention on a particular feature in the room, such as paintings, sculpture or a collection of ornaments.

Task lighting. Provides suitable light for specific activities, such as using a personal computer, watching television, reading or needlework.

Although most domestic lighting is still dependent on the conventional tungsten bulb, it's well worth familiarizing yourself with the different kinds of light sources. While the notion of fluorescent light might bring to mind any number of unattractive institutional applications, when used sympathetically and recessed behind a pelmet or

cornice, it can prove suitable for general background use, especially in a contemporary setting. Fluorescent lamps cannot be dimmed, which does tend to limit their use.

Low-voltage tungsten halogen lights are undeniably more expensive than other types of lighting but the beautiful quality of clear, white light far outweighs any disadvantages they may have. It is the closest one can get to natural daylight with an artificial light source. Low-voltage halogen lamps are now available in a wide variety of fittings — desk lights, uplighters, downlighters and spotlights, to name but a few. However, don't forget that all low-voltage lights require a transformer to step the voltage down from 240V. In the case of recessed ceiling lights there is usually one transformer per light, which is hidden in the ceiling void.

So if a fault ever occurs, only that individual transformer needs to be replaced. Surface-mounted track lights, however, often have the transformer attached to one end of the track, which can detract from its otherwise streamlined appearance. One of the advantages of low-voltage lighting is the fact that any heat produced by the bulb passes through the back of the reflector. This means that the light beam is far cooler than conventional lighting — certainly a bonus if valuable paintings are being lit.

Despite their relatively short lifespan and poor energy efficiency, tungsten filament bulbs are still the most popular and widely available form of light bulb. You can buy them in a wide range of sizes and colours; with one tinted pink or yellow you can add to the impression of warmth, or to emphasize cooler colours select a pale green or blue tint.

Remember that the colour chosen for the walls and ceilings has an important bearing on the amount of additional

light needed – while pale walls reflect light, opaque darker surfaces absorb it and stronger artificial light is required.

When shopping for light fittings you will need to bear in mind what sort of light the lamp will provide. You might

find a particular design immensely appealing to look at, but the actual light effect it produces could prove

 unsatisfactory for certain tasks. Make a study of the many different types of fittings on

offer in specialist lighting shops before you come to a decision. By using a

combination of fittings it's possible to create a flexible lighting

system that can dramatically change the mood of the room

without compromising the more functional aspects of your lighting requirements. Single,

central ceiling lights hanging from a flex do nothing to improve a room. A chandelier is a very

different matter, especially when the level of light is controlled with a dimmer. Other forms of ceiling

lighting that adapt well to most styles of decoration are low-voltage downlighters and wall-washers. Downlighters

either provide general pools of light or pinpointed circles, depending on the angle of the beam in the reflector. Wall-

washers are useful if you want to highlight a collection of prints or drawings. Spotlights can be mounted on a variety

of surfaces and are adjustable: for example, they can be used to focus attention on a particular painting or work of

 art. Uplighters provide an effective form of background or ambient light by projecting a

wide band of light onto the walls or ceiling, which is then reflected back into the room. By

throwing the light upwards, you emphasize the height of the room.

Wall lights are available in any number of styles. Sconces can prove ideal for period-

style rooms but make sure such a light is fitted with a dimmer switch, as the bulbs are often left unshaded and the

light can appear harsh. Work or task lighting contributes enormously to making your living room an enjoyable and

relaxing setting for work and study – reading in poor light results in eye strain and a lack of concentration, just as light reflected on a computer or television screen becomes a constant source of irritation. If the technicalities seem bewilderingly complex, think about obtaining advice from a lighting consultant. Many will provide the initial consultation free of charge. From the many fittings and options available they should be able to solve any lighting problem.

The installation of new wiring should of course be undertaken before you decorate, hence the importance of working out exactly where each fixed lighting point is to be located. Once you've decided how the room is going to be arranged, work out how you wish the room to be lit, according to the time of day and its various functions. Draw a clear, measured floorplan and elevation of each wall for your electrician, showing exactly where you wish points and switches to be positioned. If you leave the decisions to him, he will inevitably choose the easiest option, not the one that is most convenient or appropriate for you. Don't make the mistake of underestimating the number of power points that you will need. Extra ones are easy and inexpensive to install at the initial stages, but when added as an

8

afterthought with surface-mounted cable they hold little decorative appeal. At this planning stage it is

important to separate the power circuit from the lighting circuit. The lighting circuit controls those fittings such as ceiling lights and table lamps that will be operated from the room switch. The power circuit allows for appliances that draw more power, such as hi-fi units, vacuum cleaners and computers.

It is of course possible to give any room an instant facelift simply with the addition of one or two well-chosen lamps. Low-voltage floor and table lights may cost rather more than the tungsten equivalent, but when linked to a dimmer they can transform the appearance of the room. Though they are somewhat pricey, when you decide to move on, the lights move with you. Another ploy is merely to substitute new lampshades for tired or dated ones, making sure you resist any temptation to play dull and safe.

Unusual lamps add instant character and individuality to a room. Below: A pair of gilded wall brackets either side of this overmantel mirror would have been the conventional choice, but the startling shape of these two modern lamps bring this room right up to date. Right: modern materials and design are combined in this amusing yet practical table lamp. A highly decorative object in its own right, it provides a diffused form of background lighting.

Both these table lamps make a strong style statement. Left: Against a simple, panelled background the modern, turned wooden lampbase is well balanced by the shape and colour of its parchment shade. The smooth, sculpted angles make a striking contrast teamed with a antique leather chair and a period table. Above: The gilded lamp base and plain cream shade is a perfect choice for this side table with its decorative arrangement of classical artifacts.

Below and right: Pale cream walls and matching curtains maximize the feeling of space in lighting designer Sally Storey's London home. Superfluous decoration has been kept to a minimum in this coolly restrained classical interior. By day the room is bathed in softly suffused daylight but by night the more dramatic aspects of the room, such as the handsome pair of urns and the alcove display shelves, are brought into focus by using low-voltage halogen wall-washers, uplighters and downlighters.

The dramatic potential of this beautiful bow-fronted living room is fully exploited in the rich colour scheme — deep yellow walls and curtain fabric in the same striking tones are teamed with a sofa that is covered in a strongly contrasting stripe in shades of deep red. The unusual shape of the room is echoed in the global design of the chandelier from Kevin McCloud. For dining, the more intimate atmosphere created by candlelight is generally preferred.

A pair of tall lamps links the various elements in this symmetrical arrangement, which has been created by Sally Storey. A trio of decorative armorial prints, window- mounted in one frame, are illuminated from below by the lamps, which are fitted with a dimmer switch in order to regulate the level of light. The severity of this monochrome arrangement is counteracted by the bright red bunch of tulips and by the tiny flowerpots filled with roses.

Top: A pair of brass wall sconces balances the decorative arrangement as well as contributing to the romantic atmosphere of the London flat belonging to interior designer David Hare. Stronger light comes from the parchment-shaded table lamp. Above: The tapered lines of the lamp base echo those of the carved wooden wildfowl that is displayed alongside. Left: A star-spangled lamp forms the centrepiece of this decorative table-top arrangement.

Wall-mounted swing-arm lights are excellent providers of reading light and can be used in any number of situations, doing away with the need for a surfeit of lamp-bearing, occasional tables. Positioned at a height of around 130cm/50in from the floor, they cast a good light over reading matter without glaring into the eye. In this commodious arrangement, the lights contribute to the balance of the room as well as providing light for readers sitting on the day-bed.

Above: Rosy-red walls prove an excellent backdrop for this richly coloured collection of cushions. A pair of plain black lamps, fitted with decorative printed shades, is positioned on the table behind the sofa to supply general background lighting for this informal sitting room. Top: Chandeliers such as this simple wrought iron version can look spectacular when lit up at night with candles. Especially effective when hung above a dining table, the candle light adds to the sparkle of glass and cutlery.

This classical table lamp perfectly complements the painted decoration of the black and ochre Regency daybed. The lamp's height and handsome proportions are a prominent feature in the corner of the room and provide reading light as well as contributing a certain amount of background lighting. The plain pleated shade is the only unpatterned surface in this amusing and unconventional room with muralled walls and abundance of richly coloured fabric.

Variations on a traditional theme are demonstrated in this classically simple, symmetrical arrangement of table, lamps and painting. Given a clean, pared-down contemporary feel by the use of modern materials, the black metal table and polished steel shades are in perfect harmony with the boldness of the unframed figurative work. The strength of both the colour and subject matter against the white background makes a striking impression.

Directory

PAINTS

Dulux, Tel. 01753 550555 for details of nearest stockist. Recently introduced wide range of Heritage colours divided into Georgian, Victorian, Edwardian and Art Deco colours. Available through the Definitions tinting system in both interior and exterior paint finishes.

Farrow & Ball, Uddens Trading Estate, Wimborne, Dorset, BH21 7NL. Tel. 01202 876141. The National Trust range of 57 historical colours including Ointment Pink, Dead Salmon and a very useful Off-White. Available in seven paint types including distemper.

Fired Earth, Tel. 01295 812088. Range of eighteenth- and nineteenth-century colours developed in conjunction with the V & A Museum.

John Oliver, 33 Pembridge Road, London W11 3HG. Tel. 0171 221 6466. Long-established shop specializing in wallpapers, has an excellent range of hand-mixed paints in six different finishes including exterior masonry and floor paint.

J T Keep (Bollom), 13/15 Theobalds Road, London WC1 8SN. Tel. 0171 242 0313. Also at 314/316 Old Brompton Road, London SW5 9JH. Tel. 0171 370 3252. High-quality paints, varnishes and scumble glaze for paint finishes.

Paint Library, 2/25 Draycott Place, London SW3 2SH. Tel. 0171 823 7755. Fax 0171 823 7766. (Phone for stockists. Palette of 92 colours and glazes in various finishes including fine cement paint.)

Paint Magic, Jocasta Innes, 79 Shepperton Road, London N1 3DF. Tel. 0171 354 9696. An exclusive range of wall emulsions in subtle colours is available in Jocasta Innes's Colour Collection. The shop also stocks a range of decorative paint finish kits, specialist brushes, etc.

Papers and Paints, 4 Park Walk, London SW10 0AD. Tel. 0171 352 8626. Stocks Sanderson paint as well as their own two excellent ranges – Historical Colours and Traditional Colours. Varnishes, brushes, scumble and pigments.

Pinebrush Products, Stockingate, Coton Clanford, Stafford ST18 9PB. Tel. 01785 282799. Hand-mixed range of paints in muted colours with a flat chalky finish.

Upstairs, 38 North Street, Sudbury, Suffolk CO10 6RD. Tel. 01787 376471. The Paint Library is a range of 92 hand-mixed paints and glazes. The paints are available in emulsion, eggshell and gloss together with corresponding undercoats.

WALLPAPERS & FABRICS

Alexander Beauchamp, Vulcan House, Stratton Road, Gloucester, GL1 4HL. Tel. 01452 384959. Hand-printed wallpapers and fabrics as well a new range of Stripes & Damasks introduced to complement traditional buildings.

Anna French, 108 Shakespeare Road, London SE24 0QW. Tel. 0171 737 6555. Range of complementary fabrics, wallpapers, borders and cotton lace, many of which are based on Victorian designs.

Arc Prints, 103 Wandsworth Bridge Road, London SW6 2TE. Tel. 0171 731 3933. Amusing *trompe-l'oeil* panels of bookshelves and new range of fabrics based on eighteenth-century vogue for print rooms.

Baer & Ingram, 273 Wandsworth Bridge Road, London SW6 2TX. Tel. 0171 736 6111. Useful shop with display panels of wallpaper samples arranged according to colour. Sells wallpapers produced by different manufacturers as well as their own Fanfare range based on fleur de lys, which can be seen at selected showrooms around the country.

Beaumont & Fletcher, 98 Waterford Road, London SW6 2HA. Tel. 0171 384 2642. Fabrics based on eighteenth-and-nineteenth century European historical documents. Faded linens and richly patterned chenilles.

Bennison Fabrics, 16 Holbein Place, London SW1W 8NL. Tel. 0171 730 8076. Faded, muted and beautifully aged-looking fabrics ideal for English country-house look.

Borderline Fabrics, 1 Munro Terrace, London SW10 0DL. Tel. 0171 823 3567. Recent designs inspired by Kashmiri and Chinese patterns are printed on finest wool.

Chelsea Textiles, 7 Walton Street, London SW3 2JD. Tel. 0171 584 0111. Embroidered fabrics in the style of the eighteenth and nineteenth centuries. Also needlepoint fabric available by the metre.

Ciel Decor, 187 New King's Road, London SW6. Tel. 0171 731 0788. Specializes in traditional Provençal-style fabrics including range from Les Olivades. Table linen as well.

Cole and Son. As above. Extensive range of 1,500 historical, hand-printed wallpapers to choose from including Pugin's designs for the House of Commons. Also fine traditional fabrics.

Colefax and Fowler, 39 Brook Street, London W1Y 2JE. Tel. 0171 493 2231. Tel. 0181 874 6484 for nationwide stockists. Also at 110 Fulham Road, London SW3 6RL. Tel. 0171 244 7427. Traditional English eighteenth and nineteenth century chintzes and wallpapers and interesting range of upholstery fabrics.

Colony, 56 Hasker Street, London SW3 2LQ. Tel. 0171 589 0642. (Trade only but phone for stockists.) Sumptuous woven fabrics – brocades, damasks and lampas from Italy.

De Gournay, 14 Hyde Park Gate, London SW7 5DG. Tel. 0171 823 7316. Hand-painted chinoiserie wallpapers.

The Design Archives, P O Box 1464, Bournemouth, Dorset BH4 9YQ. Tel. 01202 753248. (Phone for stockists: trade only.) Fabrics and wallpapers reproduced from period archives and documents.

Designers Guild, 267/271 & 277 King's Road, London SW3 5EN. Tel. 0171 243 7300. Shop and the adjacent showroom are filled with bright ideas for wallpapers and fabrics as well as contemporary-style upholstered sofas and chairs.

Gainsborough Silk Weaving Co. Ltd, Alexandra Road, Sudbury, Suffolk CO10 6XH. Tel. 01787 372081. (Phone for stockists. Trade only.) Fine woven fabrics in the traditional manner.

Hodsoll McKenzie, 52 Pimlico Road, London SW1 8LP. Tel. 0171 730 2877. Fabrics, wallpapers, trimmings and furniture. Eighteenth-and nineteenth-century style.

Ian Mankin, 109 Regent's Park Road, London NW1 8UR. Tel. 0171 722 0997. also 271 Wandsworth Bridge Road, London SW6 2TX. Tel. 0171 371 8825. Good-value checks, stripes, tartans, and plains in Indian cotton. Mail order service.

Ikea. Tel. 0181 208 5600 for nearest branch. Excellent value for furniture, fabrics and accessories. Contemporary styles in the main but some re-working of traditional themes.

Jane Churchill, 151 Sloane Street, London SW1X 9BX. Tel. 0171 730 9847. Tel. 0181 874 6484 for nationwide stockists. Wide range of fabrics – prints, sheers and upholstery in traditional style but with a strong contemporary feel. Wallpapers and trimmings as well.

Laura Ashley, 256 Regent Street, London W1. Tel. 0171 437 9760. (Tel. 01628 622116 for nearest branch.) Extensive range of fabrics, wallpapers and paints.

Liberty and Co. Regent Street, London W1. Tel. 0171 734 1234. Distinctive florals as well as a new collection of Arts and Crafts designs.

Lewis & Wood at Joanna Wood, 48a Pimlico Road, London SW1 8LP. Small collection of coordinating linen unions, cottons, muslins, linings and wallpaper.

Mikhail Pietranek, Saint Swethin Street, Aberdeen, AB1 6XB. Tel. 01224 310211. Baronial Home collection was inspired by Scottish tartans. Scottish glen checks are produced in cotton as well as wool. Also complementary paisley and floral designs.

Mrs Monro, 16 Motcomb Street, London SW1X 8LB. Tel. 0171 235 0326. English floral chintzes and unions at their best.

Nice Irma's, 46 Goodge Street, London W1P 1FJ. Tel. 0171 580 6921. Varied collection of ethnic fabrics from India including crewel work by the metre. Good for Tudor-style rooms.

Nina Campbell, 304/308 Kings Road, London SW3 5UH. Tel. 0171 352 1456. (Tel. 0171 675 2255 for nationwide stockists.) Wide range of classic prints, weaves and trimmings.

Nordic Style at Moussie, 109 Walton Street, London SW3 2HP. Tel. 0171 581 8674. Reasonably priced Scandinavian-style fabrics, furniture and accessories.

Nouveau, Queen's Road, Doncaster, South Yorkshire DN1 2NH. Tel. 01302 329601. (Trade only but phone for local stockists.) Very reasonably priced collection of prints and weaves based on historical designs.

Osborne & Little, 304/308 King's Road, London SW3 5UH. Tel. 0171 352 1456. Tel. 0181 675 2255 for local stockists. Fabrics, wallpapers and trimmings in a wide range of styles, displayed in spacious showroom.

Pukka Palace, 174 Tower Bridge Road, London SE1. 3LS Tel. 0171 234 0000. Very reasonably priced range of Indian cottons.

Sanderson, 112/120 Brompton Road, London SW3 1JJ. Tel. 0171 584 3344. Extensive range of fabrics and wallpapers. Known for their collection of William Morris designs.

Stuart Renaissance Textiles, Barrington Court, Barrington, Nr Ilminster, Somerset TA19 0NQ. Tel. 01460 240349. Part of Stuart Interiors, specialists in all aspects of furnishing interiors from medieval times to the seventeenth century. Fabrics are contemporary woven copies of English and European museum pieces.

Sussex House, 92 Wandsworth Bridge Road, London SW6 2TF. Tel. 0171 371 5455. Small range of exclusive fabrics based on the designs of antique textiles.

Timney Fowler, 388 King's Road, London SW3 5UZ. Tel. 0171 352 2263. Distinctive contemporary designs based on classical architectural motifs.

Watts of Westminster, 2/9 Chelsea Harbour Design Centre, London SW10 OXE. Tel. 0171 222 2893. Victorian style at its grandest – some designs by Pugin. Fabrics, wallpapers and trimmings.

FURNITURE: CONTEMPORARY

Aero, 96 Westborne Grove, London W2. Tel. 0171 221 1950.

Amadeus, 309a King's Road, London SW3 5EP. Tel. 0171 376 4435.

Art in Iron, Imperial House, Townmead Road, London SW6. Tel. 0171 384 3404. Stocks range of wrought-iron furniture and will also undertake commissions.

Authentics, 20 High Street, Weybridge, Surrey KT13 8AB. Tel. 01932 859800.

Camp Classics, 24a Sydney Street, Brighton, East Sussex BN1 4EN. Tel. 01273 689389.

The Conran Shop, 81 Fulham Road, London SW3 6RB. Tel. 0171 589 7401.

Heal & Son, 196 Tottenham Court Road, London W1. Tel. 0171 636 1666.

Muji, 26 Great Marlborough Street, London W1V 1HL. Tel. 0171 494 1197.

Purves & Purves, 80/81 & 83 Tottenham Court Road, London W1. Tel. 0171 580 8223.

Richard Taylor Designs, 91 Princedale Road, London W11 4SN. Tel. 0171 792 1808. Decorative metal furniture hand-made in Europe.

Ruth Aram, 65 Heath Street, London NW3 6UG. Tel. 0171 431 4008.

Suzanne Ruggles, P O Box 201, London SW7 3DL. Tel. 0181 542 8476 for appointment. Bold, elegant furniture in hand-forged metal. Neo-classical, Empire and Baronial collections.

FURNITURE: ETHNIC

David & Charles Wainwright, 251 Portobello Road, London W11. Tel. 0171 727 0707. Also 28 Rosslyn Hill, Hampstead, London NW3. Tel. 431 5900. Interesting and unusual Indian furniture and accessories.

Global Village, 249 Fulham Road, London SW3. Tel. 0171 376 5363. Furniture and accessories including rugs.

Nice Irma's, 46 Goodge Street, London W1P 1FJ. Tel. 0171 580 6921. Smaller items of furniture, rugs and accessories.

Pukka Palace, 174 Tower Bridge Road, London SE1 3LS. Tel. 0171 234 0000. Colonial-style Indian furniture.

William Sheppee, 1 Church Avenue, London SW14. Tel. 0181 392 2379. Antique Indian furniture and a range of reproductions in colonial style.

FURNITURE: TRADITIONAL SOFAS & CHAIRS

A Barn Full of Sofas and Chairs, Furnace Mill, Lamberhurst, Kent. Tel. 01892 890285. Phone for appointment. Range of newly made, comfortable Victorian- and Edwardian-style sofas, as well as a selection of antique and second-hand sofas and chairs.

George Smith, 587 King's Road, London SW6 2EH. Tel. 0171 384 1004. Over-sized sofas a speciality. Very comfortable and stylish and will undertake upholstery in kelims, of which they have a good selection in stock.

Kingcome Sofas, 302/304 Fulham Road, London SW10 9EP. Tel. 0171 351 3998. Range of handsome, traditionally made sofas. Will undertake special commissions.

The Odd Chair Company, 66 Derby Road, Longridge, Lancashire PR3 3FE. Tel. 01772 786262. Good stock of individual period chairs including Victorian.

Sofa & Co. High Green, Great Shelford, Cambridge. CB2 5EG. Tel. 01223 843500. Sofas supplied with washable loose covers.

The Sofa Factory, 15 Tunsgate, Guildford, Surrey GU1 3QT. Tel. 01483 455464. Phone for brochure. Branches in Brighton, Kingston and Henley.

TRADITIONAL FURNITURE & ACCESSORIES

Artisan, Unit 4a, Union Court, 20 Union Road, London SW4 6JP. Tel. 0171 498 6974. (Mail order service available, phone for catalogue.) Decorative ironwork for curtain poles, door and window fittings and bedsteads.

Clock House Furniture, The Old Stables, Overhailes, Haddington, East Lothian EH41 3SB. Tel. 01620 860968. Range of stools of every size and design. Standard range as well as one-off items.

Country Desks, 86 High Street, Berkhamsted, Hertfordshire HP4 2BW. Tel. 01442 248270. Range of desks including copy of early Victorian pedestal desk with space for filing.

The Desk Depot, 274 Queenstown Road, London SW8 3ND. Tel. 0171 627 3897.

Just Desks, 20 Church Street, London NW8 8EP. Tel. 0171 723 7976. Excellent range of antique and reproduction desks. Also special home computer desks with facilities for hiding wires.

The Dorking Desk Shop, 41 West Street, Dorking, Surrey RH4 1BU. Tel. 01306 883327. Large selection of antique desks and writing tables to choose from.

Holbein, Wrafton Works, Rear 45 Evelyn Road, London SW19 8NT. Tel. 0181 542 2422. Range of highly decorative hand-painted accessories including curtain tassels, finials, poles and lamp bases.

Laura Ashley By Post, P O Box 5, Newtown, Powys SY16 1WW. Tel. 01800 868100. Everything in the Laura Ashley Home catalogue from lampshades to sofas is available by post.

Lloyd Loom Direct Ltd, P O Box 75, Spalding, Lincolnshire PE12 6NB. Tel. 01775 725876.

Monica Pitman Collection, G5 Chelsea Harbour Design Centre, Chelsea Harbour, London SW10 0XE. Tel. 0171 376 3180. Range of metal furniture, lighting and accessories inspired by eighteenth-and nineteenth-century antiques.

Shaker, 322 King's Road, London SW3. Tel. 0171 352 3918. Traditional Shaker-style furniture and accessories.

Upstairs, 38 North Street, Sudbury, Suffolk CO10 6RD.

Tel. 01787 376471. Filoseat and Casseat are stools with inbuilt storage space for files, cassettes and clutter.

FIREPACES & FENDERS

Acres Farm, Hungerford Lane, Bradfield, Reading, Berkshire RG7 6JH. Tel. 01734 744305. Club fenders in a range of styles and sizes. Also made-to-measure.

Farmington Stone, Farmington, Northleach, Glos GL54 3NZ. Standard range as well as made-to-measure limestone fireplaces.

Spirestone, Hollis Lane Top, Chesterfield, Derbyshire S41 7RA. Tel. 01246 221714. Traditional, made-to-measure, hand-carved stone fireplaces.

Walcot Reclamation, Walcot Street, Bath, Avon. Tel. 01225 444404.

LIGHTING

The London Lighting Co Ltd. 135 Fulham Road, London SW3. Tel. 0171 589 3612.

Christopher Wray, 600 King's Road, London SW6 2YW. Tel. 0171 736 8434. Huge decorative lighting store. Has regional branches in Birmingham, Bournemouth, Bristol, Leeds, Manchester and Nottingham.

John Cullen Lighting, 585 Kings Road, London SW6 2EH. Tel. 0171 371 5400. Contemporary lighting specialists.

McCloud & Co. 269 Wandsworth Bridge Road, London SW6. Tel. 0171 371 7151. Stylish lighting and accessories.

Mr Light, 275 Fulham Road, London SW10. Tel. 0171 352 7525. Also 279 King's Road, London SW3. Tel. 0171 352 8398. Contemporary, unusual designs.

Richard Taylor Designs, 91 Princedale Road, London W11 4SN. Tel. 0171 792 1808. Range of decorative lamps, chandeliers, wall lights in seventeenth-and eighteenth-century styles.

FLOOR COVERINGS

Acar Antiques, 340a King's Road, London SW3. Tel. 0171 376 5279. Fabulous collection of kelims and interesting antiques. Will upholster using kelims.

Crucial Trading, The Market Hall, Craven Arms, Shropshire SY7 9NY. Tel. 01588 67666. Phone for details of stockists. London showroom at Pukka Palace, 174 Tower Bridge Road, London SE1 3LS. Tel. 0171 234 0000. Comprehensive range of natural floor coverings.

Fired Earth, Twyford Mill, Oxford Road, Adderbury, Oxordshire OX17 3HP. Tel. 01295 812 088. Tiles, rugs and natural jute, seagrass and coir flooring.

Roger Oates Design Associates, The Long Barn, Eastnor, Ledbury, Herefordshire. Tel. 01531 632718. Phone for stockists. Stylish carpets and jute.

ACKNOWLEDGEMENTS
The publisher should like to thank the following sources for providing the photographs for this book:
Robert Harding Picture Library/IPC Magazines 29 top, 46 left, 48 bottom, 55, 62 bottom, 66 bottom, 81 bottom/**Jan Baldwin** 6 bottom, 7 centre, 10 top, 16, 22 left, 26, 31 top, 39, 45, 50 centre, 63 centre, 64 top & centre, 65 top, 68 top, 72, top, 74, 87 top/**David Barrett** 6 centre, 12 centre & bottom, 13 centre, 21, 29 centre, 79 bottom, 89 top/**Tim Beddow** 7 bottom, 8 top, 11 middle, 13 bottom, 19 left, 27 top, 48 top, 56 bottom, 67, 81 centre/**David Brittain** 47 bottom/ **Simon Brown** 9, 27 bottom, 49 bottom, 60, 68 bottom, 77 left, 78 bottom, 87 bottom/**Richard Davies** 70/ **Christopher Drake** 12 top, 18 left, 19 right, 23 bottom, 33, 34, 42, 50 bottom, 56 top, 78 centre, 90/ **Michael Dunne** 38, 48 centre, 54 top, 71/**Clive Frost** 88/**Lu Jeffrey** 20/**Ken Kirkwood** 49 top, 91/ **Simon Lee** 10 centre, 30 centre/**Tom Leighton** 28 centre, 69 top, 87 centre, 89 bottom/**Mark Luscombe White** 36 top, 49 centre/**Nadia Mackenzie** 8 bottom, 23 top, 78 top, 79 top & middle, 82, 83 left/**John Mason** 50 top, 53 bottom/**James Merrell** 13 top, 22 right, 24, 31 centre & bottom, 43, 47 top, 59, 64 bottom, 65 centre & bottom, 66 top & centre, 76, 77 right, 80 top & bottom, 83 right, 84, 86/ **Jonathan Pilkington** 53 top, 58, 61/**Trevor Richards** 10 bottom, 14, 15, 28 bottom, 30 bottom, 41, 46 right, 81 top, 85/**Paul Ryan** 7 top & centre, 62 top & centre, 63 bottom, 73/**Andreas von Einsiedel** 11 top & bottom, 17, 18 right, 30 top, 35, 44, 51 bottom, 57, 63 top, 75/**Polly Wreford** 6 top, 28 top, 32, 36 bottom, 37.

Andreas von Einsiedel 25, 29 bottom, 40, 54 bottom, 69 bottom, 72 bottom

Christopher Wray's Lighting Emporium 80 centre